Garlic: Powerful Healer!

by Karolyn A. Gazella

This booklet is intended for educational and informational purposes only. Please see a qualified healthcare professional if you have questions about your health.

Design by Linda Busby, Brainchild Designs

Published by:
IMPAKT Communications, Inc.
P.O. Box 12496
Green Bay, WI 54307-2496

Dedication

This booklet and everything good that I do is dedicated to the loving memory of my mom, Eunice Gazella. May her warmth and kindness live on through me and the many others she influenced.

How's Your Health?
An IMPAKT Communications Health Series

The *How's Your Health?* booklet series by IMPAKT Communications is designed to provide you with accurate, up-to-date information on using natural medicine as a part of a comprehensive health program. This series highlights important topics that are thoroughly researched and written by highly qualified physicians, researchers, and health writers. Visit your local health food store, pharmacy, or health clinic to find out more about this educational series, or call 1-800-477-2995 (U.S.), 1-888-292-2229 (Canada). Quantity discounts are available. For more information about other booklets, books, and magazines published and distributed by IMPAKT Communications, refer to the back of this booklet.

Contents

Introduction

I just love garlic. Unfortunately, after I eat a lot of garlic, those around me don't love me!

It's been called the "stinking rose," as it is best known for its odor; however, the far-reaching medicinal benefits this herb provides make it as beautiful as a rose. It is probably one of the most widely studied foods of our time.

Here are the key therapeutic uses of garlic:

- Cardiovascular—including lowering blood pressure and cholesterol levels.
- Cancer—as a preventive or to reduce or eliminate cancerous tumors and protect the body during conventional cancer treatment.
- Antiviral, antifungal, antibacterial, antioxidant, and possibly for weight loss and diabetes.

In addition to using garlic as a treatment for these conditions, possibly the most important use for garlic is in the area of prevention. Adding fresh garlic to your daily diet, or taking a quality dietary garlic supplement will do wonders to stimulate your immune system and keep you healthy. Some health experts even believe garlic has some anti-aging effects—probably due to its impressive positive influence on the immune and cardiovascular systems.

While garlic is a very important herb for our health, it is a very complex botanical. It can be difficult sifting through all of the garlic rhetoric. Alliin, allicin, allinase, etc., etc. The ABCs of garlic can sometimes sound like a different language.

This booklet will help peel away the layers of confusion, revealing a wealth of solid, scientific evidence that will help you choose the right garlic product. You will learn what to look for in a garlic product and why. You will learn the importance of reading the label and how to determine a quality product, just by looking at the label.

I know first-hand about the confusion, because I was once confused too! When my sister was diagnosed with breast cancer, we searched for information about the products that would best fit her situation. I knew garlic should be a part of the treatment plan, but I wasn't sure which garlic product she should take.

This booklet provides details about what I learned during my search for the right garlic product. I wasn't about to just have her take any garlic—after all, it was her life we were trying to save!

Fortunately, when I was operated on for ovarian cancer, the research was already done. Today, I take garlic everyday to help prevent my cancer from returning.

As the publisher of three international natural health magazines, I am fortunate to be associated with some of the finest, most respected healthcare professionals throughout the world. I also have the opportunity to talk with people on a regular basis who read our books and publications. Their stories of tragedy and triumph are emotionally stirring. I have heard first-hand about the many benefits of garlic and I am motivated by their success stories and touched by their sheer determination.

Garlic. Something so simple yet so powerful. We are blessed to have access to this incredible herbal substance. It has been in the past and will remain in the future, one of our most treasured natural medicines. This booklet will help you experience the true power of this wonderful botanical. But first, a caution…

This booklet is designed to give you scientific information regarding the many benefits of garlic. While serious illnesses such as cancer and heart disease will be mentioned, it is important to remember:

If you are experiencing health problems, consult your physician for proper diagnosis and treatment options. Do not self-diagnose.

The information in this booklet is educational only. It is not designed as medical advice.

A Historical Perspective

Garlic has a rich history steeped in anecdotal success. Dating back as far as 1550 B.C., Egyptian records show garlic as an effective remedy for a variety of illnesses.

In 1609, Sir John Harrington wrote about this "stinking rose" in *The Englishman's Doctor*:

"Garlic then have power to save from death
Bear with it though it maketh unsavory breath,
And scorn not garlic like some that think
It only maketh men wink and drink and stink."

Probably most notable was Pasteur's use of garlic as an antibiotic in 1858 and Albert Schweitzer's success treating dysentery in Africa and as an antiseptic in the prevention of gangrene during World Wars I and II.

According to *The Healing Power of Herbs* by Michael T. Murray, N.D., "In 1721, during a widespread plague in Marseilles (France), four condemned criminals were recruited to bury the dead. The gravediggers proved to be immune to the disease. Their secret was a concoction they drank, consisting of macerated garlic and wine...and it is still available in France today."

Beginning with the Egyptians and moving to the Greeks and Romans, garlic made its way through history treating a plethora of ailments. From tooth fillings to surgical disinfectants, garlic got the job done.

"Truly, garlic has seen some interesting and unusual applications within the course of human history," writes John Heinerman, Ph.D., in his book, *The Healing Benefits of Garlic*. Dr. Heinerman refers to garlic as one of the oldest medicines of our time.

As modern research "catches up" with history, we are discovering that there is more to garlic than just folklore. While historical use lets us know that garlic has been used safely for centuries for a variety of illnesses, today's medicine requires a more scientific approach. Garlic is surely up for such scrutiny as there have been approximately 2,000 scientific published papers documenting its powerful effects on the prevention and treatment of disease. Very serious illnesses are finding a worthy opponent in this simple (yes, and stinky) herb.

Especially of interest to the scientific community are garlic's immune-enhancing properties. Due to the effect garlic has on the immune system, it shows great promise in the area of cancer prevention and treatment.

Cancer Prevention and Treatment

Cancer is a very complicated condition. Despite more than three decades of a concentrated "war on cancer," we are no closer to a cure and have made little progress in the area of conventional treatment. By the year 2000, experts believe two in five people will develop some form of cancer in their lifetime. It's no wonder individuals with cancer look to alternatives in the area of treatment and prevention.

My sister and I know what it's like to be faced with this serious illness. We have combined conventional treatments with natural medicine to give us the most comprehensive plan of attack possible.

While garlic supplements are by no means a cure or a panacea, garlic can provide incredible support to your immune system. Obviously, the best way to deal with cancer is to prevent it from occurring in the first place. Garlic can be a powerful weapon in your anti-cancer arsenal.

Some of the most important studies regarding garlic consumption and cancer are known as epidemiological, or studying populations. The textbook, *Garlic: The Science and Therapeutic Application of Allium sativum L. and Related Species* edited by Heinrich P. Koch, Ph.D., M.Pharm., and Larry D. Lawson, Ph.D., expertly outlines the various studies on garlic and also provides a very scientific review of this fascinating herb.

While there are several studies confirming the therapeutic benefits of garlic on specific types of cancer, here are some of the more recent:

- A comparison of two counties in the same province in China indicated very different garlic eating habits. An epidemiological study of the counties showed that the county where fresh garlic is consumed more frequently had a significantly lower incidence of stomach cancer.
- Also in China, 564 patients with stomach cancer and 1,131 other people living in an area with a high rate of gastric cancer experienced significant benefit by eating fresh garlic. People eating the most garlic and Allium foods had a 60 percent less chance of developing cancer than those who ate the least amount of garlic.
- The "Iowa Women's Health Study" featured 41,387 women who were monitored for colon cancer for a five-year period. It was most notable that garlic was the only food which showed a statistically significant association with a decrease in colon cancer.

In addition, many animal and test-tube studies exist clarifying the role garlic plays in the area of cancer prevention and treatment. Clearly, garlic is becoming one of the most studied food substances of our time.

According to the garlic textbook by Drs. Koch and Lawson, "...it is apparent that the anticancer effects of garlic are likely due, perhaps equally, to both allicin or allicin-derived compounds as well as to unidentified compounds not related to allicin."

A key reason garlic is so powerful against cancer is due mostly to its antioxidant effects. Free radicals enter our bodies on a daily basis through the air we breathe, the foods we eat, and the water we drink. Free radicals can damage cells causing them to become cancerous. Antioxidants protect cells from free radical damage. That's why substances such as garlic are so important in the treatment and prevention of cancers.

At this point, epidemiological studies show garlic is most beneficial for stomach and colon cancers; however, animal studies have shown it to be beneficial for breast, liver and other cancers.

Keep in mind, the most successful cancer treatment and prevention plan will feature the following:

- a healthful low fat, high fiber diet
- regular exercise
- nutritional support through supplementation
- mind/body techniques

Garlic is surfacing as a key herb to help prevent and treat cancer. Important compounds found in garlic will actually prevent cancerous cells from forming.

In addition to being a powerful antioxidant, garlic has also been shown to actually enhance immune system activity by stimulating B and T cells. As a matter of fact, in a human study involving seven AIDS patients, there was a major increase in the percentage of natural killer cell activity.

In another study, elderly patients were given 600 mg of a garlic preparation standardized for alliin/allicin (we'll discuss this more in a later chapter). In these people, there was a significant increase in the immune system's ability to kill the E. coli bacteria.

There are 54 billion white blood cells in our body just waiting to gobble up viruses, bacteria, germs, and cancer cells. Our immune system has an incredible power to kill these cancer and other toxic cells. When stimulated and kept healthy, our immune system can protect us from illness. Scientific research has confirmed that garlic is a very powerful immune stimulating herb.

Garlic to a white blood cell is like spinach to Popeye! Feed your cells what they need and they'll be healthy and strong.

Heart Disease

While cancer is on the rise, heart disease remains the number one disease killer in the United States. Heart disease and all of the other illnesses that can lead to heart disease, including high blood pressure and high cholesterol, can be a very frightening experience. Fortunately, there are many steps you can take to prevent and treat heart disease. Garlic is among the key natural medicinal products that has shown incredible benefit in the area of enhanced cardiovascular health.

Just as with cancer, there are no "magic bullets" to shoot at this dangerous enemy. A truly comprehensive approach to prevention and treatment includes many factors including lifestyle changes in diet and exercise activity. Fortunately, garlic and other natural substances such as vitamin E, cayenne, and hawthorn extracts can provide important additional support.

“The modern use of garlic has focused on its ability to lower cholesterol and blood pressure in the attempt to reduce the risk of dying prematurely from a heart attack or stroke,” explained Dr. Michael Murray in *The Healing Power of Herbs*. “The majority of studies showing a positive effect of garlic and garlic preparations are those that delivered a sufficient dosage of allicin.”

While we will go into more detail about dosage and type of garlic in a later chapter, let’s first take a closer look at the recent studies on the benefits of garlic for the heart.

“Of all the effects of garlic that have been reported over the years, perhaps the most interesting are those on the heart and circulatory system,” according to Hans D. Reuter, Heinrich P. Koch, and Larry D. Lawson. “…development of arteriosclerosis can be prevented or an already existing condition favorably influenced.”

One of the most important articles on garlic was published in the *Annals of Internal Medicine* (October 1993) confirming garlic’s ability to lower total cholesterol levels. While this study showed a decrease of at least nine percent, which is significant, many other studies indicated a 15 to 20 percent drop in levels.

A recent study from Kuwait showed that participants who ate three grams of garlic every morning for 16 weeks had a 21 percent decrease in serum cholesterol. The length of the study is important as no significant decrease was found after four weeks.

Tulane University School of Medicine in New Orleans was the site of a study using garlic to lower cholesterol. The results were published in the June 1993 issue of the *American Journal of Medicine* and showed that after 12 weeks, total cholesterol dropped by six percent and LDL (“bad cholesterol”) was reduced by 11 percent. “The fact that this study was conducted in the United States is significant as most research on garlic’s cardiovascular benefits have been previously conducted in Europe with much of the other garlic research coming from Japan and other parts of Asia," explained Mark Blumenthal, executive director of the American Botanical Council.

"Although garlic's effects on cholesterol levels are not phenomenal, the combination of lowering LDL and raising HDL can greatly improve the LDL to HDL ratio—a significant goal in trying to prevent heart disease and strokes," according to a research report in *Health Counselor* (February/March 1995).

Garlic has also been studied for its ability to lower blood pressure. In addition to lowering blood pressure, many studies found there was a significant improvement in the secondary effects of high blood pressure such as headache, dizziness, insomnia, and indigestion. A general sense of well-being was also consistently reported.

Fairly recently, a drug-monitoring study of 1,997 patients with high blood pressure also indicated that garlic can lower blood pressure. In this study, average blood pressure went from 146 over 85.5 to 140.5 over 82.5; however, there was an even more distinct benefit in those individuals with mild hypertension who were not on any medications.

Please remember that if you are on blood pressure medication, you should not discontinue use without consulting your physician. High blood pressure is a very serious illness requiring the care of a qualified healthcare professional.

Lowering cholesterol and blood pressure are key benefits offered by garlic. It has also been discovered that garlic can prevent the formation of toxic derivatives of cholesterol by acting as an antioxidant. In addition, garlic prevents the excessive clumping together of blood platelets, which if left unchecked, can lead to heart disease. This is known as platelet aggregation.

"Garlic, like aspirin, inhibits platelet aggregation," according to *The American Journal of Natural Medicine* (October, 1995). "However, garlic possesses several additional protective actions against heart disease…these additional effects are simply not observed with aspirin."

These are all important benefits for individuals trying to prevent or treat cardiovascular illness. People with a strong family history of heart disease will especially benefit from garlic—either by increasing the amount of garlic in the diet or supplementing the diet with "odorless" garlic tablets.

The scientific community is taking notice of garlic's positive effects on the cardiovascular system. In October 1995, researchers from the United Kingdom, Germany, Russia, United States, and Canada presented impressive confirmation regarding the extensive benefits garlic has on the cardiovascular system. Published studies regarding garlic's ability to lower cholesterol and blood pressure were presented at this conference, the Berlin Garlic Symposium of the 6th Annual Phytotherapy Congress held in Germany.

"The symposium on garlic is further documentation of the scientifically validated cardiovascular benefits of this increasingly popular traditional herbal remedy," concluded Blumenthal.

Garlic is an important and powerful medicine for our cardiovascular system. By lowering blood pressure and cholesterol, garlic can help ensure your heart will stay healthy and continue pumping for years to come. What's even more attractive is that garlic can provide therapeutic benefit to those individuals with heart problems or a family history of heart disease.

Other Uses

It is becoming very clear why garlic is one of our most widely studied foods—because it provides such important medicinal benefits.

While tackling America's number one and two disease killers is no small task, garlic clearly can benefit people trying to prevent and treat these serious illnesses. But, it doesn't stop there. As if heart disease and cancer aren't enough, garlic also has other important applications.

Scientific evidence as well as anecdotal accounts, tell us that garlic can be used to treat or prevent the following:

- diabetes
- viruses, bacteria, and parasites
- fungi (i.e. Candida albicans)

Antimicrobial/Antibacterial

"Garlic exerts a broad-spectrum antimicrobial activity against many genera of bacteria, virus, worms, and fungi as summarized in several works," explained Dr. Murray. "These findings seem to support the historical use of garlic in the treatment of a variety of infectious conditions."

Regarding garlic's antibacterial activity, several studies have compared it to commonly used antibiotics like penicillin, streptomycin, and others. "Besides confirming garlic's well-known antibacterial effects, the studies demonstrated this herb's efficacy in inhibiting the growth of some bacteria that had become resistant to one or more of the antibiotics," according to *The Healing Power of Herbs*.

In addition, garlic is also very resistant to germs and helps prevent the formation of toxins produced by microorganisms. Allicin, which is found in garlic, has also been shown to actually enhance the effectiveness of some antibiotics.

Antifungal Agent

Garlic is also very powerful against fungi—the most significant being Candida albicans. "From a clinical perspective…both animal and test tube studies have shown garlic to be more potent than nystatin, gentian violet, and six other reputed antifungal agents," explained Dr. Murray.

A vivid illustration of garlic's intense antifungal properties comes from a major hospital in China. At this hospital, garlic therapy alone was used successfully to treat cryptococcal meningitis, which is one of the most serious fungal infections imaginable.

Again, it was allicin in garlic that was shown to be responsible for the anticandida activity of garlic in test tube studies. Many human studies have confirmed garlic's impressive anticandida and overall antifungal activity.

Antiviral Activity

Regarding antiviral effects, much historical and anecdotal evidence exists to show garlic can assist the body when under attack by a virus. Test tube and animal studies have confirmed this effectiveness. Of specific interest to researchers is the effect garlic has on the HIV virus and influenza.

Intestinal parasites is also a key area of interest to garlic researchers. It is believed garlic can help prevent the establishment of intestinal parasites, especially roundworm and hookworm. While the broad effects garlic has as a parasitic treatment is unknown, allicin is believed to be the most active compound within garlic against parasites.

Complementary Diabetes Treatment

Diabetes rounds out the list of conditions that will benefit from garlic. While the effects of garlic on diabetes has not been studied nearly as much as cancer and heart disease, there are some benefits diabetics will receive from garlic.

Garlic has been shown to decrease blood sugar levels, which is of utmost importance in diabetics. "The mechanism by which garlic affects blood sugar appears to be either its ability to stimulate the pancreas to increase insulin production, make protein-bound insulin physiologically available, or positively affect blocked cell membrane insulin-receptors, or some combination of the above," according to *Garlic: Nature's Perfect Prescription*.

In one animal study done in India, garlic was almost as effective at controlling blood sugar levels as insulin or other prescription drugs. Keep in mind, however, that you should never discontinue medication without proper supervision from your doctor.

Garlic is completely safe. Adding it to the diabetic diet just may be a good idea.

Anti-aging

With all of the good things that come from eating garlic or supplementing the diet with garlic, it's no wonder that researchers are now discovering it will help you live longer and much healthier.

One researcher in Denmark has even shown through test tube studies that garlic has anti-aging activity. Human skin cells were placed in laboratory dishes. Varying amounts of garlic extract was added to each of the dishes. The skin cells were monitored while they reproduced. According to the research article featured in the *Journal of Ethnopharmacology*, the cells that were supplemented with the most garlic lived significantly longer and were much healthier than the cells not receiving garlic.

Animal studies at the University of Tokyo confirmed the laboratory results. The Tokyo study also found that the animals receiving the garlic lived significantly longer than those not receiving garlic. It was also noted that learning ability and memory was also improved in the garlic-supplemented group.

Garlic "…might be useful for treating physiological aging and age-related memory deficits in humans," concluded the Tokyo researcher.

Because garlic can bolster the immune system, keep the cardiovascular system strong, and treat infections, it's no wonder people who take it live long. As a powerful antioxidant, garlic will work on many levels to keep you strong and healthy for a long time.

Now that we know all of the great things garlic can do for us, let's take a closer look at why it works.

Analyzing Garlic

One of the most confusing and controversial aspects about garlic is what makes it work. This is an important issue. If we don't know what makes it work, we don't know what to look for when we are buying garlic products. And if we don't buy the most effective product, we won't get the therapeutic benefit. And if we don't get the benefit, we are wasting our time and money, and even more importantly, jeopardizing our health!

If you discuss garlic with six different people, chances are they will all agree about the many benefits of garlic; however, unfortunately, you will probably get six different answers as to what makes garlic work. And that's because garlic is a complicated substance.

Garlic contains a variety of sulfur compounds. It is believed that more than 90 percent of the investigations regarding garlic focus on these sulfur compounds. This is due to the many benefits these sulfur components offer. There is significantly more sulfur in garlic than any other food source. Sulfur provides many therapeutic benefits. In fact, drugs such as penicillin and antibiotics contain sulfur. It has been shown that if you eliminate a class of these sulfur compounds known as thiosulfinates, which allicin is the most abundant source, you also remove all or most of garlic's antibacterial effects.

While allicin is a very key component of garlic, it is also very unstable. Allicin is responsible for garlic's strong odor. Have you every wondered why garlic in the clove, harmlessly sitting on your kitchen countertop has no odor and yet, once you cut or crush it, the scent builds? When you cut the garlic clove, an important enzyme, known as allinase, reacts with alliin to form allicin, causing a smelly "scentsation" (pun intended).

As soon as the allicin is released through the cutting or crushing, it becomes a very unstable molecule, changing and breaking down within hours. The challenge is in getting the full benefit of the allicin before it breaks down and becomes useless.

As we have seen, in many of the studies, allicin has been shown to be the therapeutic active compound in garlic. As a matter of fact, the German Kommission E, an expert panel of physicians, toxicologists and pharmacists that regulate herbal products according to the same strict principles as pharmaceuticals, also feels products that provide the most allicin are the most beneficial.

Allicin is a pretty fickle molecule. Scientists call it unstable. Once allicin is released by cutting or crushing, it's lost within a few hours at room temperature or a couple of days if it's refrigerated. Heat also stops the process and depletes allicin completely from garlic. In addition, allicin cannot be measured in the blood because it reacts with different molecules to form other compounds.

While alliin is not responsible for the therapeutic effects of garlic, it is necessary to create allicin. So, let's get this straight: alliinase is an enzyme that reacts with alliin to form allicin, which is the key medicinal compound in garlic.

That makes sense; however, there is a "catch 22." We know that it takes a reaction between allinase and alliin to create allicin. Unfortunately, that reaction occurs when the garlic is cut or crushed, causing the allicin to become very unstable, beginning a breakdown. So, how can we get the benefits of allicin (which we know we need in order to receive the true medicinal effects of garlic displayed in the studies)? Is the only way to eat whole, fresh garlic everyday, or is there a nutritional supplement that can provide us with the allicin we need?

Leave it to the Swiss!

The Swiss Patented Process

After years of investigation, Swiss researchers discovered a way to extract and separate the alliin from the allinase. This separation takes place when the material is wet before the reaction takes place. The material is then dried. The final substance is a highly standardized amount of alliin from fresh garlic.

But wait…without the allinase, there is no allicin—which is what we're looking for! Realizing this, the researchers then mix the dried allinase with the dried alliin and put it in an enteric-coated tablet. When the tablet becomes wet and breaks down in the body, the allinase reacts with the alliin and allicin is formed, providing the medicinal benefits achieved in the studies.

The process is so revolutionary, the Swiss researchers were granted a patent for their innovative technique—patent number 5,176,913.

Here are the key benefits achieved with the Swiss patented process:

- The product is standardized so each and every capsule has guaranteed potency for consistent results.
- The amount of allicin released per tablet can be guaranteed because of the process used.
- The enteric-coated tablet ensures the garlic does not break down in the stomach, but is delivered to the gut where it can be absorbed.This also means odor-free breath.

In addition to all of these benefits, the Swiss process is literally able to pack the tablet with the most allicin per tablet possible, creating the highest potency garlic supplement available worldwide. It only takes one of the patented Swiss tablets to get 4,000 mg of fresh garlic and 5,000 mcg of allicin, which is the amount recommended by the German Kommission E, a government agency that evaluates the safety and effectiveness of herbal products.

This special Swiss patented product is available in the United States, Canada, Germany, Austria, and France. Visit your local health food store or pharmacist, or ask your natural medicine provider for details.

With all of the new information and advanced technology becoming available regarding garlic, it is vital to know how to choose the best product. Next, let's evaluate what to look for in a product and how to analyze the label.

Choosing the Right Product

Because many of us don't like to eat whole, fresh garlic every day, we need to rely on nutritional supplements to provide us with the benefits of garlic without the odor. While there are dozens of garlic products to choose from, choosing the right one can be challenging.

To get the best results from your garlic product, you will want to match the studies as close as possible regarding dosage. "Based on a great deal of clinical research, the dosage of a commercial garlic product should provide a daily dose of at least 10 mg of alliin or a total allicin potential of 4,000 micrograms," according to *The Healing Power of Herbs*. This is equal to about 4,000 mg of fresh garlic.

Because allicin is so important, the most effective product

will state a guaranteed amount of allicin production. Be aware of the subtle techniques manufacturers of garlic products use to label their products.

For example, many manufacturers will claim a very high "total allicin potential." Upon closer examination of the label, the words, "at time of manufacture" can be found in very small print. Remember what we learned about allicin? Within hours of any activity (cutting, crushing, heating) it begins to break down.

When those words appear on the label, it means the product is not stable and the manufacturer does not guarantee the level of allicin (the most important component of the garlic) at the most critical time—when the product is actually used. The level of alliin or the total allicin potential at the time of manufacture is meaningless.

Basically, there are two types of garlic extracts available, fresh and aged, and a third garlic product, dried powder.

Dried garlic powder manufacturers simply dry the sliced garlic and encapsulate the material. Unfortunately, to reiterate again, whenever you slice garlic, the allicin is activated and changes. That's why manufacturers of dried garlic powder products can only guarantee allicin content at the time of manufacture.

Aged means the garlic is cut up, the material is fermented in alcohol for 20 to 24 months and then is encapsulated. Here again, we have the same problem—cutting and fermentation is not good for allicin. Aged garlic products will not release any allicin in the body, but will destroy it in the fermentation process.

Using a supplement that is made of fresh, unharmed garlic is the best possible choice. Most of the epidemiological studies and many of the clinical studies used fresh, whole garlic that was eaten. While this is preferred, eating a clove of garlic every day may not be the most aromatic or feasible alternative.

Supplements supplying fresh garlic, standardized for allicin and alliin content, are the most effective products available. Make sure the level of alliin and the total allicin potential is clearly stated on the label. Chances are, the more descriptive the label, the higher quality the product.

There are a variety of forms of garlic. While the most common is odorless (deodorized) garlic tablets or capsules, here are a few other ways you can find garlic:

- a tea (also referred to as a decoction)
- fluid extract (tincture)
- juice
- oil
- liniment or ointment
- suppository

As you can see, there are a variety of uses and delivery systems for garlic. People are anxious to receive the healing benefits from garlic and are utilizing it for all types of health concerns. Because garlic in the form of a dietary supplement is the most common, let's take a closer look at how to analyze a garlic supplement label to ensure you get the best product possible.

Looking at the Label

"The modern use of garlic features commercial preparations designed to offer the benefits of garlic without the odor," explained Dr. Murray. "The marketplace is swamped with garlic products, with each manufacturer claiming their product is the best."

Sifting through information and discerning fact from fiction is up to you. Here are some tips as to what you should look for in a garlic product label:

- Description. The more information you can gain from the packaging of a product, the more comfortable you will feel about taking it.
- Guarantee. A manufacturer that guarantees the product is confident and quality-conscious.

- Certificate of Analysis. This document should be presented by an independent laboratory stating what the levels of each compound are in the product.
- Quality manufacturing process. The patented Swiss process yields the most effective, highest potency product in the world.
- Standardization. This ensures that each capsule or tablet is consistent, which will provide the results you are looking for.
- Dosage. Look for a product that will give you 4,000 mg of fresh garlic and 5,000 mcg of allicin.

At the Berlin symposium on garlic held in October 1995, standardization was emphasized with the researchers concluding, "Positive and, above all, reproduceable therapeutic results can only be expected from standardized proprietary medicinal garlic products."

Standardization for a specific active component is so important when dealing with herbal products. This guarantees each and every capsule or tablet contains the same amount of active ingredient, which provides you with the most effective, consistent results.

Follow these recommendations and remember to buy a product that most closely provides you with what was used in the studies. This will ensure you get the most benefit from your garlic supplement.

Remember, the real thing is always preferred. "In addition to the use of garlic preparations, garlic consumption as a food should be encouraged, despite its odor, in patients with high cholesterol levels, ischemic heart disease, hypertension, diabetes, candidiasis, asthma, infections (particularly respiratory tract infections), and gastrointestinal complaints," recommends Dr. Murray.

Toxicity and Side Effects

We know that garlic is effective, but is it safe? Just as with many natural substances, garlic is very safe. That's what makes it such an appealing medicine.

"For the vast majority of individuals, garlic is nontoxic at the dosages commonly used," according to Dr. Murray.

Some people may develop irritation to the digestive tract. In animal studies, prolonged feeding of large amounts of garlic resulted in anemia, weight loss, and failure to grow.

"Although the exact toxicity of garlic has yet to be definitively determined," concluded Dr. Murray, "side effects are rare at the dosage recommended." The dosage Dr. Murray recommends coincides with many of the studies and is 10 mg of alliin or a total allicin potential of 4,000 mcg daily. This is equal to 4,000 mg of fresh garlic. Because individual needs may vary, it's best to consult with your pharmacist, natural healthcare provider, or health food store, for more information.

More is not necessarily better. Garlic seems to provide excellent therapeutic benefit at the dosage described.

Several studies, as featured in the textbook on garlic edited by Drs. Koch and Lawson, describe very large amounts of garlic with no toxicity. In one study, 200 people consumed 15 grams of garlic daily (about 15 cloves) for three and one-half weeks with no side effects.

In one China province, the average daily consumption of fresh garlic is about five cloves. While this province has a very low incidence of stomach cancer, Dr. Koch believes, "This is probably near the upper limit of a safe level of garlic consumption, although it is expected that cooked garlic, which contains no or little allicin, could be safely eaten in considerably higher amounts."

So, as it is true that toxicity levels have not been established, garlic has been shown to be completely safe at the recommended dosages.

A Quick Review

It's difficult not to get excited about this unassuming little herb. Considered one of the most studied foods of our time, the scientific community is discovering the many medicinal benefits garlic provides.

Steeped in history, garlic is not just for vampires anymore! Anecdotal evidence is becoming confirmed and people throughout the world are receiving the many benefits of garlic.

Not surprisingly, with all of this excitement, there is a glut of garlic products on the market. People are turning to nutritional supplements because they are trying to avoid the pungent odor of garlic. There's no denying, garlic is "strong" in many respects.

I have good friends who love to eat at their favorite neighborhood Italian restaurant. Garlic is in practically everything! The food is delicious and the portions are plentiful. There's only one problem. If they take their leftovers home, their entire house will smell like garlic for days after.

I find that same result when I cook with garlic in my home. Although the garlic odor hangs around for a few days, I wouldn't have it any other way. It's one of my favorite seasonings!

How fortunate we are that something so tasty is so good for us!

Garlic is a powerful healer that will help prevent and treat cardiovascular illness and cancer. It can also be used to prevent and treat viruses, bacteria, and fungi (like candida). Diabetics may also find benefit by including more garlic in their diet or by taking a garlic supplement.

While the physiology and terminology regarding garlic can be confusing, it is clear, based on the studies, that allicin is the most important factor. Here are some general tips to follow when choosing a garlic supplement:

- learn as much as possible about the product you are considering
- read the label carefully and choose a product with a descriptive label
- choose a product that guarantees potency and quality

Don't rush into your purchase. You don't want to waste your valuable time and money by using an inferior product. Most of all, you want to be sure to get the most effective product possible. After all, we are talking about our health!

Final Thoughts

When my sister and I got cancer, we were scared. We wanted to do everything we could to get rid of our cancer and prevent a recurrence.

I'm here to tell you that garlic did not save our life—but it was a part of the plan—a plan that includes dietary changes, increased exercise, supplements to stimulate the immune system, and a positive mental attitude.

I have seen the devastation of cancer and other serious illnesses. That's why it is so exciting to see a natural substance, such as garlic, providing such incredible benefits and backed by such strong scientific documentation. The positive studies on garlic are extensive. There are even symposiums and festivals devoted just to garlic.

When I was deciding what garlic supplement to use, I read labels and sifted through the information that was presented. I finally settled on a product that uses the patented Swiss manufacturing process. It was very appealing to me to be able to get the recommended amount of garlic in one tablet. You can only imagine the amount of supplements I take in an effort to prevent my cancer from coming back. The last thing I wanted was to take more supplements.

Compared to the one tablet of the patented Swiss product, it would take nine tablets of another leading garlic brand. I wasn't about to add nine more tablets to my daily routine. The one-a-day garlic was the answer for me.

Today, it's been nearly two years since my cancer surgery and nearly three years since my sister's diagnosis. We are doing fantastic and we continue to take our garlic tablet each and every morning. In addition, I incorporate fresh garlic into my diet whenever possible.

The scientific research has now confirmed what the pharaohs, philosophers, and gladiators knew a long time ago: A clove a day keeps the doctor away. It will keep your immune and cardiovascular system healthy and protect you from viruses, bacteria, and fungi. And that will prove to be the tip of the iceberg. Look for science to prove garlic provides even further medicinal benefits. It truly is a powerful healer!

Books by IMPAKT

- Beating Cancer with Nutrition by Patrick Quillin, Ph.D. (Paperback, 254 pages) $16.95
- Breast Cancer by Steve Austin, N.D., and Cathy Hitchcock (Paperback, 336 pages) $18.95
- Childhood Illness and the Allergy Connection by Zoltan Rona, M.D. (Paperback, 256 pages) $16.00
- DHEA: A Practical Guide by Ray Sahelian, M.D. (Paperback, 158 pages) $11.95
- Encyclopedia of Natural Medicine by Michael T. Murray, N.D. (Paperback, 622 pages) $21.95
- Encyclopedia of Nutritional Supplements by Michael T. Murray, N.D. (Paperback, 564 pages) $21.95
- Flax for Life! by Jade Beutler (Paperback, 96 pages) $7.95
- Getting Well Naturally Series by Michael T. Murray, N.D.
  - Menopause, 182 pages
  - Diabetes and Hypoglycemia, 164 pages
  - Male Sexual Vitality, 150 pages
  - Chronic Fatigue Syndrome, 196 pages
  - Arthritis, 158 pages
  - Stress, Anxiety, and Insomnia, 178 pages

$10.95 each or all six for $60.00

- Ginger: Common Spice and Wonder Drug by Paul Schulick (Paperback, 166 pages) $11.95
- Healing Power of Herbs by Michael T. Murray, N.D. (Paperback, 410 pages) $17.95
- Heal Yourself Naturally edited by Karolyn A. Gazella (Paperback, 200 pages) $16.95
- Help Yourself: The Beginner's Guide to Natural Medicine by Karolyn A. Gazella (Paperback, 134 pages) $10.95
- Melatonin: Nature's Sleeping Pill by Ray Sahelian, M.D. (Paperback, 144 pages) $15.95
- Natural Alternatives for Weight Loss by Michael T. Murray, N.D. (Hardcover, 157 pages) $22.00
- Natural Alternatives to Over-the-Counter and Prescription Drugs by Michael T. Murray, N.D. (Hardcover, 383 pages) $30.00
- Natural Alternatives to Prozac by Michael T. Murray, N.D. (Hardcover, 222 pages) $22.00
- Preventing and Reversing Osteoporosis by Alan Gaby, M.D. (Paperback, 304 pages) $16.95
- Seven Keys to Vibrant Health by Terry Lemerond (Paperback, 113 pages) $12.95

- Take Charge of Your Body by Carolyn DeMarco, M.D. (Paperback, 296 pages) $19.95

- The Vitamin Revolution in Health Care by Michael Jansen, M.D. (Hardcover, 236 pages) $24.95

- Total Wellness by Joseph Pizzorno, N.D. (Hardcover, 419 pages) $24.95

- Understanding Fats and Oils by Michael T. Murray, N.D., and Jade Beutler (Paperback, 74 pages) $6.95

To order any of these books, visit your local health food store, pharmacy, or natural healthcare provider. Or call IMPAKT Communications at 1-800-477-2995 (U.S.) or 1-888-292-2229 (Canada). VISA, MasterCard, American Express, and Discover accepted. You can also call to receive a complimentary listing of all the books published and distributed by IMPAKT.

FREE Information!

Do you have an interest in other health topics from a natural medicine perspective? Choose from any one of these topics and receive a **FREE** article reprinted from *Health Counselor* magazine. **Only one article per household.**

Simply check which topic you are interested in, fill out the form below and mail this page to:

IMPAKT Communications
P.O. Box 12496
Green Bay, WI 54307-2496

- ❑ Cimicifuga extract (black cohosh): A natural alternative to estrogen for menopause.
- ❑ Kava: Nature's answer to anxiety.
- ❑ Natural alternatives to Prozac and other antidepressants.
- ❑ Natural alternatives to ulcers.
- ❑ Bovine cartilage: Panacea or placebo?
- ❑ Preventing cold sores and herpes outbreaks.
- ❑ PCO Sources: Grape seed vs. pine bark
- ❑ Questions and answers about DHEA.
- ❑ Saw palmetto: Nature's answer to enlarged prostate.

Name ____________________________________

Address ____________________________________

City/State/Zip ____________________________________

Phone ____________________________________

About the author

Karolyn A. Gazella is the president and founder of IMPAKT Communications, Inc., an international magazine and book publishing and distribution company. She is the publisher of *Health Counselor*, *Health Security*, and *The American Journal of Natural Medicine* magazines. Karolyn is the author of *Help Yourself: The Beginner's Guide to Natural Medicine* and has recently edited the book, *Heal Yourself Naturally*. She is also the author of the booklet, *Thymus: Master Gland of Immunity!*, which is part of the *How's Your Health?* series through IMPAKT Communications.